The Music Keeps on Playing

The Music
Keeps on Playing

by
Audre Pitts

Beacon Hill Press of Kansas City
Kansas City, Missouri

Copyright 1988
by Beacon Hill Press of Kansas City

ISBN: 083-411-2507

Printed in the
United States of America

Cover Design: Crandall Vail

All Scripture quotations are from *The Holy Bible, New International Version,* copyright © 1973, 1978, 1984 by the International Bible Society, and are used by permission.

10 9 8 7 6 5 4 3 2 1

CONTENTS

The Music Never Stopped	7
I Hate Escalators	10
"I've Got You Under My Skin"	12
Büsingen Invasion	15
Gesundheit	25
When Is Garbage Not Garbage?	28
Here Comes the Dreamer	31
Jinx?	33
I'm a Coupon Clipper	36
People Are My Hobby	38
Some Mornings Are like That	43
The Age of Wrinkles	45
2 Chronicles 20:21	48
The Confessions of a Collector	50
Things That Go Bump in the Night	52
I'm Not the Only One	54
I Like Rain	58
Number One Chicken	60
Bowl 'em Over!	62
I Can't Blame It on Old Age	64
Gweneth	70
I've Looked Everywhere	74
I Like Apartment Living—But	77
Just a Scribbler	80
Yesterday, Today, and Tomorrow	84
P.S.—All Cruisin', No Boozin'	87

The Music Never Stopped

When I was still a preschooler our family lived in the little village of Jamestown, Kans. Across the street from our house was a vacant lot where the traveling carnival set up when it came to town. It was a small show, and the only ride was the big beautiful merry-go-round. I'd never seen one, and I still remember the thrill of riding on it! Papa thought I was too young to ride on one of the horses, so I rode in the chariot. Even now the sound of carousel music sends my mind flying back over time, and I savor again in memory the joy of those rides.

Many years later I was traveling with my sister and brother-in-law and their young son. Whenever we came to a town where there was a merry-go-round he begged to ride on it, without success.

When we got to Utah where my brother and his family lived they took us to an amusement park on the shore of Salt Lake. We rode out from town on an electric trolley. It jiggled and joggled, teetered and tottered, shivered and quivered, and shuddered and swayed. It jerked and jolted the passengers until we were bouncing around like Mexican jumping beans. What made it even crazier were the mirrors around the inside that reflected all of this wild action. We laughed ourselves silly.

When we got to the park, of course there was a merry-go-round. Again Charles coaxed to ride but no one wanted to ride with him, and he was too small to go by himself. Listening to the haunting strains of the carousel music that had lived in my mind and heart all those years I couldn't bear for him to be disappointed.

"Come on, Charles," I said, "I'll ride with you."

I wasn't content to stand beside him on his horse. I clumsily mounted one of my own and settled myself for a long, nostalgic journey. What resulted was a ludicrous ride. My poor beastie was overloaded! Instead of going gracefully up and down as did all the others, it painfully and slowly inched itself up, up, up to the top. Then—kerplop! It dropped suddenly to the bottom.

But my brave little steed never gave up. Again and again it jerkily made its way to the top—with the same spine-jolting drop each time. The onlookers were enjoying my ride as much as I. Maybe more.

Life is something like a merry-go-round. I've gone around in circles sometimes—enjoying the ride and the music but not traveling far. I've had my ups and downs, and I've raced my motor when I couldn't accomplish my goals as quickly as I wanted. I've grabbed for the brass ring now and then. A few times I've caught it.

I've also had some heart-jerking jolts when it seemed as if my life had suddenly been yanked out from under me. But my Father was always there to help me back up on my little horse again. And, through it all, the music never stopped playing.

The music keeps on playing
 Deep down within my soul,
Whether skies above are sunny
 Or clouds of sorrow roll. . . .

The music keeps on playing
 And makes my heart to sing,
For the music that I am hearing
 Is the voice of Christ, my King!

I Hate Escalators

We were on our way to Australia and running late. As we dashed toward the Air New Zealand gate at the Los Angeles International Airport I came to a quick halt at the top of an escalator.

Down, down, down went my friend Kent with his and my carry-on luggage. But I stood in frozen panic.

"Come on," he shouted, looking back.

"I can't, I can't," I wailed, waggling my hands helplessly.

His eyes held mine coldly as he sternly asked, while still in swift descent, "Do you want to go to Australia?"

Before I could say, "No, not if I have to go by escalator," Judy, one of the girls in the group, put her arm around my shoulder. With me clinging to her like a drowning person, we rode down together.

For the rest of the trip we walked miles (I'm sure) upstairs and downstairs so we wouldn't have to go through that scene again. I finally learned to, very clumsily, ride *up* on one of the contraptions—with help. So that eliminated some of the stairs.

When a Work and Witness team from our church went to Europe later that year I almost did it again. We were rushing through the air terminal when I was again confronted by a runaway staircase, and I didn't dare stop. I was in a foreign country and didn't want to be stranded by myself. I frantically clutched a girl who was rapidly dropping away from me and sailed along with the gang. From then on whoever was nearest to me was my lifeline.

I'm awkward enough riding on a moving walkway. It's the on and off process that almost throws me. Stepping on a walk that is running away from me is hard enough when it is on the level. But when it is running away from me *downhill,* it is downright risky business. I lose my poise, my equilibrium, and my courage.

I think escalators remind me too much of a slippery slide in the park that I played on as a child. My two sisters, my cousin, and I went there one summer evening. It had rained earlier in the day, but the weather had cleared.

I ran ahead so I could be the first one down the slide. A common practice among some of the bolder children was to slide down on a piece of waxed paper to make the descent more swift and exciting. I had never been that brave, but someone else had been just before I got there.

I clambered up the steps, got myself in position, and started down. The slide wasn't straight—it had "waves" in it. I hit the first wave and from then on I never even touched the slide. I flew through the air (but not with the greatest of ease) and landed in a mud puddle at the bottom.

My new dress and I were a mess! To make matters worse I had to walk several blocks back home wearing a mud plaster on my backside.

I never had the courage to go on one again. My motto is, "If it moves downward, keep off!"

"I've Got You Under My Skin"

I seem to be the type of person who attracts bloodsucking insects. Mosquitoes love to gorge themselves on my blood. And wood ticks are simply fascinated with me.

On our first trip to Oregon from Kansas years ago I picked up one of the little "suckers." We were in a motel near Portland after having driven up the Columbia Gorge until late the night before. When I awoke that morning I felt a stinging sensation in the back of my leg just above the knee.

Brushing my hand against it I discovered something foreign there. At my excited shriek, my husband came to life. He found the tick right away. I'd heard of them but had not previously made the acquaintance of any.

"Yank it out, yank it out!" I yelled. He yanked and ended up with just its body in his grasp. The head was still embedded.

Later we arrived at the home of his sister and brother-in-law in Portland and, in the busy whirl of reunion, we forgot about it until evening.

As we were visiting I told them what had happened. Doris said, "I don't want to scare you, but people die from tick bites."

Her husband, Harry, came up with a remedy that he had heard was effective in treating such things. He said to fill a small bottle with boiling water, then empty it and put the mouth of the bottle against the bite. The hot vapor was supposed to draw out the poison.

I couldn't see the place, so Raymond took over the first aid treatment. But he forgot to empty the boiling water from the bottle before applying it to the bite. I stood there and howled with surprise and pain while they *scalded* me.

I was ready to let it end right there. But just as I crawled into bed, he said, "You know, just to be sure, I think you should put some turpentine on that place." Turpentine was his stock remedy for everything. For a cold he used turpentine and lard on his chest. He also used turpentine for all cuts and scratches. Now it was tick bites.

Obediently getting back out of bed, I dipped some cotton in turpentine and, reaching behind me, rubbed it on the spot. Oh murder, oh misery! I only *thought* it had hurt before.

He didn't think it could be all that bad, but he looked. The boiling water had made a blister and it had broken. I had rubbed that fiery turpentine on a raw burn!

After that I steadfastly refused any more of his tender and well-meaning (but decidedly amateur) ministrations of mercy. Live or die, I was through being tortured.

Other times I have found ticks on my clothing after being in the woods. But that was the only time one ever personally attacked me.

Mosquitoes—ticks—and, in Australia, leeches. Our new Aussie friend, Judy, had taken us for an outdoor barbecue on Mount Tambourine. After we'd eaten she led us on a walk down a rain forest path. She assured us that it hadn't rained enough for leeches to be a problem.

As we were walking back up the trail she found out that they *were* a problem. One of them was nosing its way into her toe. We rushed back to the picnic site, and Kent struck a match and put the flame against the end of the leech. It made a quick backward exit, but Judy was so afraid she was going to get her toe burned off that she didn't even see it leave.

On the way home we stopped at a little tea shop. While we were at the table I said, "Maybe I'd better check *my* shoes."

I slipped off one sandal and found two leeches in it. Hastily taking off the other, I found three more! The owner, hearing our excited exclamations, told us to take them outside and put salt on them to kill them.

Judy and Kent each grabbed a shoe and a saltshaker and ran outside. I didn't have any shoes left to wear, so I stood inside and snapped pictures through the window as they frantically waged war on the leeches. There were five leeches in the sandals, but when they came back in they had only found three of them. They knew the other two were on the loose somewhere—and Kent was sure he knew where.

He took off his shoes and examined them, then his socks, and looked between his toes. He even rolled his pants above his knees and searched his hairy legs for leeches. But there were none to be found.

All the way home I imagined I could feel them crawling all over me, and the shower that I immediately took was as hot as I could stand. I even shampooed my hair. The missing leeches were never found.

Somewhere in Australia there may be two lonely little leeches still looking for me.

Büsingen Invasion

The trip to Europe was a dream come true—one I hadn't even dreamed yet. I had never expected it to happen.

Arriving at our first hotel in Germany I was interested in the difference between their bedding and what I had always known. I was used to sheets, blankets, and a spread. I had never seen a bed cover that looked like a flat feather bed snapped inside a sheet covering.

That night I was the last one in bed, as usual. I switched off the light across the room and got into bed in the dark. I spent an uncomfortable night. My legs ached, and I didn't seem to have room to move them.

When the alarm woke us next morning I mentioned my discomfort to my roommate. Jan looked over at me and started laughing.

"No wonder you couldn't sleep," she said. "You crawled down inside the covering!"

I looked and sure enough, I'd been cramped up inside that envelopelike covering all night long. No wonder I couldn't find room to move my legs.

Lesson No. 1 for Audre: When in Germany sleep *under* the feather comforter not *inside* it.

There were 44 men and women in the group sent from our church. To the students and faculty it might have looked more like an invasion than a Work and Witness team. We swarmed over that campus. We acted as painters, carpenters, plumbers, upholsterers, and seamstresses. One person was in charge of the laundry, and 44 people can dirty a lot of clothes in a week.

They can also eat a lot of food and dirty a lot of dishes. That's where some of us came in. Some helped cook, others washed dishes, and others helped in the dining room. That is where I worked, along with another. Besides our 44 there were the students and faculty along with their families. A number of the students are married. There were three babies born to students during the week we were there.

* * *

At the college five of us were assigned to a two-room apartment. The night before, when we had stayed at the hotel in Erlensee, two of us were branded as heavy breathers—snorers in fact.

It was decided that we two should share the living room and the other three would sleep in the bedroom. They thought, by closing the door, they would be protected from the sound of our snoring. But we fooled them. We didn't have a door to close, and theirs wasn't enough to shut out our nightly onslaughts. Their door may have deadened the sound a bit. But I am sure that their consensus would be, "Not much!"

* * *

Besides the week we spent at the European Nazarene Bible College, which was rich in fellowship, we also had opportunity for some trips. Our Sunday afternoon cruise up the Rhine was something I will always remember. The college is located across the street from the river, so we didn't have far to go to the boat landing. Even though it was a showery day we all enjoyed it. I kept remembering the stereoscopic slides I had viewed as a child, especially the ones showing pleasure boats on the Rhine. And here we were. But our ladies were not wearing long white ruffled gowns and wide-brimmed hats like the ladies in the slides. We wore slacks and donned rain hats whenever a sudden shower came upon us.

Our boat landed at Stein-am-Rheim, an ancient Swiss village. There was a tiny church there where Zwingli (the Swiss Protestant reformer) had preached. The pulpit from which he delivered his sermons many years ago is still there. In the church there is a stone statue of Christ before which he had often knelt. Zwingli always said that the only way a person could look into the eyes of Christ in the statue was from a kneeling position.

On one end of a building across the street from the church was an ancient mural of Zwingli preaching to the people.

The antiquity of all the buildings and bridges was a fascination for Americans with an urban renewal complex. On the boat trip we passed under a bridge that was built hundreds of years ago.

* * *

The little village of Büsingen has an interesting history of its own. When the Protestant reformation swept across Switzerland the residents of Büsingen voted to stay with Catholic Germany. As a result it is still a German town—but completely surrounded by Switzerland—sort of an island within a country. We were constantly crossing German and Swiss borders as we went in and out of the village.

* * *

One morning after finishing my dining room chores I slipped across the street to the riverbank. I was never able to really absorb the fact that I was actually there on the Rhine. I sat watching the swans take off so clumsily in flight and land so gracefully on the water.

An old tune from my childhood kept running through my mind. It was a World War I melody that the doughboys used to sing,

> *We don't want the bacon,*
> *We don't want the bacon,*
> *All we want is a piece of the Rhine.*

I used to listen to that on our neighbor's phonograph. (It may have been called a gramophone then. The records were cylinder-shaped.)

Rocks of all shapes and sizes interest me. My husband always said I picked out the biggest I could find to take home from an outing—and he had to do the carrying. I knew, that day by the Rhine, that there wasn't much room left in my suitcase, so I chose a very small colorful pebble from the river's edge where the water was lapping over them. I brought it with me triumphantly. At last *I* had a piece of the Rhine.

I wish I could remember where I put it after I got home.

* * *

Germany and Switzerland have a climate similar to ours in Oregon. So in October we all took our raincoats with us. I got a lot of compliments on mine from the ladies on campus and from my own teammates. It was like most others that season—sort of rose-mauve nylon. But theirs were all quite long and mine was shorter—more of a car-coat length.

In answer to their question, "Where did you find a short one? I wish mine were short," I'd answer that I just cut mine off and hemmed it. And I added that I liked it better that way.

That was the truth, and nothing but the truth. But one day I confessed to my roommates the *whole* truth. Two nights before we were to leave on our trip I was doing some practice-packing around midnight. I had put my raincoat in the zippered compartment of one of my bags. When I tried to take it out I found that part of it was caught in the zipper. I worked and worked (calling myself stupid, dumb, bird-brained, and other uncomplimentary names). Finally, I had to make a choice. It was either ruin the zipper on my new suitcase or cut a chunk out of my new raincoat.

The raincoat lost. With a tiny pair of scissors I snipped it out of the zipper. My suitcase was OK, but the raincoat had a little round hole in the back. I looked it over and decided that amputation was its only chance of survival.

So, with a large pair of scissors this time, I whacked it off just above the wound. It took me most of the night to get the hem in by hand. It was a long way around the bottom of that thing. I am not a nimble-fingered needlewoman, and when I got to the end of it, I had more material than I needed. So I just folded it neatly (?) into the corner of the hem and hoped no one would ever see it.

When I was finished with it I looked heavenward and sighed, "Lord, when You gifted me You certainly didn't gift me as a seamstress."

Little did I realize that my poor mangled, chopped-off raincoat would turn out to be so admired.

* * *

Our visit to the Rhein Falls near Schaffaeuden was more than just a trip. To me, it was an awe-inspiring experience. We went in a small boat out to the falls. Because of my ill-tempered knee I didn't attempt to climb the steps to the top with the others.

I stood on the landing and gloried in the magnificence of the falls and their thundering torrential plunge down the side of the rocky crag. The spray sloshed over me and filled my shoes with water. But I had on my raincoat, and my shoes would dry eventually.

In a sudden burst of radiance a gorgeous rainbow shone through the mist, and I felt tears flowing down my cheeks. With only the falls and their Creator as my audience, I began singing over and over the triumphant chorus "How Great Thou Art!"

Each time I came to the last phrase of the chorus I opened up all the stops and gave it full volume soprano.

My Father and I had a beautiful worship time together that sunlit October afternoon on the landing.

* * *

Another thrill was our trip to the Swiss Alps, through the town of Appenzell and on to the Santis. There we took a cable car ride to the top of the mountain. I loved it. Cable cars don't frighten me like escalators do.

Before going on the trip I had gotten some books from the public library and did a bit of reading on the area. Our schedule showed that we would be in the Appenzell region of the Alps on one of our trips. I read that the men there were short in stature.

In talking to my dental hygienist one day while she was cleaning my teeth I jokingly remarked that I should try to catch a short man there.

When I went back in a few days to get a tooth crowned she was all ready for me. She had made me a "short-man catcher kit"—a box covered with gift wrap and filled with a toothbrush, toothpaste, sugarless gum, a flower for my hair, and other interesting items.

It's just as well that I left the kit at home. We didn't stop in the town—just drove through it. Besides I wouldn't have had room for a short man in my suitcase if I'd caught one.

After our week of working at the college we toured for a week. Walter Crow, the college rector, was our tour guide. His wife, Linda, and daughter, Keli, also accompanied us. I think Linda knows every good shopping place in West Germany. We left a lot of American dollars there. I'm not as much of a shopper as some. I would walk into a store and ask if they had any music boxes. If not, I usually went on. I am a buyer, not a shopper. I tell people I am not much of a *looker*, and they can take that any way they wish.

Walking on brick and cobblestone streets didn't agree with my arthritis. Whenever my knee got too painful I'd find a place to sit down and people-watch. In Schaffhausen, Switzerland, one afternoon I was sitting on a bench in the square. A lady walked by with her little boy, of perhaps 18 months, in a cart. He was nibbling on a cookie. As they passed me he reached out and stuck it in my hand. The mother wasn't looking and walked on by, leaving me sitting there feeling like a cookie-snatcher with the evidence right in my hand.

* * *

The day we left the college we drove across the upper part of Switzerland and Austria. The weather was gorgeous, and I have never seen more beautiful scenery anywhere. To use a phrase popular with youngsters—the mountains were awesome!

The team members were so kind. Someone always offered me a helping hand or arm when there was stair-climbing involved. Such was the case when we visited the Castle of King Ludwig II on Lake Chiemsee. The sight of so much gold is fabulous. I bought a book so I could review it all later. It was simply too much for my peasant mind to absorb at the time. And just think—all of it isn't a patch on what we will see in heaven when we get there.

I will always have many beautiful memories of our European trip . . . the friendliness of the people . . . the picturesque window-boxes of geraniums in hotels, homes, business places . . . the beautiful scenery and manicured look of the fields . . . the preservation of history.

We rode over brick roads built by the Romans when Europe was part of their empire. In my imagination I could see the helmeted Roman soldiers on their prancing mounts, hear the clank of the horses' hooves—even see the sparks fly as their hooves struck the bricks. I reached back into the dim corridors of my remembrance of high school Latin classes about Caesar and his wars. But all I could come up with was, "All Gaul was divided into four parts."

I kept wondering if I was riding over roads in one of these four parts. There are still fortresses, bridges, and city walls that were built in that era. And there would be so many more had it not been for the ravages of war.

※ ※ ※

I can't leave the subject of our trip without mentioning the rapport between the members of our team. Can you imagine what it *could* have been like with 44 people living, eating, working, traveling, and shopping together for three weeks?

Ah, but I left out the most important one—worshiping together. Before work started each day at the college our people gathered in the chapel for devotions led by one of our team members, Dr. Henry Ernst. And while traveling, Walt and Linda led our devotions on the bus as we rode along.

On the last day we were all to be together, before some left us to go on further travels, we had a sharing time. It was beautiful. We laughed together, cried together, sang together, and praised God together as our bus ate up the miles.

The day before, 13-year-old Keli had livened things up for us while we were riding, by teaching us a chorus in German. We asked her to sing more and more and more. As we applauded her final song, she prankishly snatched a newly purchased Alpine hat off one of the men and pranced down the aisle, passing it to the crowd. Her father was mortified and moaned that he just might disown her. But we loved it and recklessly tossed in a conglomeration of marks, francs, shillings, and even some American coins.

※ ※ ※

On our return home, our overseas flight ended at Seattle. From there we were to take Air Alaska to Portland. We were on a tight schedule, so they hurried us through customs. Then we rushed to catch the next plane. As we left the customs area one of the men asked directions. The attendant said to get on a little electric trolley at Station A and get off at D.

We hopped on and it went to B—then shot back again to A. After two or three fruitless efforts to get to C we got off to ask more information. A young lady in uniform came over and asked if she could help. I guess we must have looked confused. I know I *felt* that way. I'd never before met a trolley car that didn't know the alphabet.

She went right along with us to that same Station A and went to B—*then* she had us get off, scuttle across a wide room to Station C. *It* went to D. Off again. From there we were to take an escalator upstairs, but only one side was working and it was crowded. So she whisked us (as fast a limping woman *could* be whisked) to an elevator. I felt that my guardian angel was really with me. I hate escalators!

Soon we were where we belonged—with no time to spare. I'm glad Paul was with me. Had I been alone I'd never have made it. I would still be shuttling from A and B and back again—seeking but never finding shuttles C and D.

I arrived home with a suitcase full of souvenirs, a mind buzzing with new sights and sounds and scenery, a heart full of memories, a body in which every joint and muscle hurt like a bad toothache—and very, very happy!

The music had never stopped playing.

Gesundheit

When our team arrived in Germany my vocabulary was limited to almost one word—*Gesundeit*. I heard someone use it in a prayer in our first Sunday morning church service there, and my first thought was "Who sneezed?"

Having been an avid reader of the Katzenjammer Kids cartoons as a child had helped me some. I found this out when I wandered into a small German cafe in Berchtesgaden by myself one day and asked for a sandwich. The man said, "No sandwich," then offered, "Sausage mit brodt?"

I smiled triumphantly and agreed, "Sausage mit brodt."

It was delicious. I love their rolls, which are so crispy on the outside and flaky and delicious inside. The sausage was what I'd call a weiner—only it was so-o-o-o good. Much better than I'd ever eaten before.

It didn't take long to learn two other words that were of great help—*Damen* and *Herren*. They were printed on the doors inside a W.C., which in our country is known as a rest room.

One rainy day while in the Bavarian Alps we stopped at the little town of Winkl. I looked in some of the shops. Then I spied a W.C. sign on a building. There was a stairway leading down into a large room with a Damen door on one side of the hall and Herren on the other. W.C. I had learned, and Damen I had learned. But as I stood in there and surveyed that long row of locked doors I groaned. Not one was free. I had some German coins, but I hadn't the foggiest idea which ones to use. There were instructions above the lock on the door. I'm sure it must have said "Deposit" something, but what? I picked one out of my hand and tried it. But it didn't work, so I tried another. It didn't work either.

Soon I heard someone coming down the steps and hoped that help was coming. It was a gentleman and when I popped out of the Damen door and eagerly asked, "Could you help me, sir?" I think I gave him quite a fright. He jumped back quickly, and I held out my handful of coins. I shrugged deprecatingly and, pointing to myself, I explained, "I'm an American," and shook my hand in confused puzzlement as I stirred the coins. I pointed to the "Damen" and ended with a pleading look. "I don't know which to use."

I couldn't speak German, but he understood my sign language and my look of helplessness. I had caught his attention with the word *American*, and he smiled indulgently as we both went into the Damen. Taking a coin from my outstretched hand, he dropped it in one of the slots and opened the door. Then, with as much gallantry as a royal coachman opening the door for Queen Elizabeth, he held it open for me to enter. And, with a courteous nod of the head, he left.

I know that ladies aren't supposed to speak to strange men, but he wasn't strange at all. He was very nice. I was the strange one. Besides there wasn't anyone around to introduce us, and the bus would soon be leaving.

✸ ✸ ✸

He was much kinder than the lady in Salzburg, Austria. Hers was a privately owned facility—sort of a basement cubbyhole, which I spied while people-watching in the square. There was one small room in which the owner lived and her customers paid to use her "other room." When I saw her the word *crone* came to mind as an apt description. She was bent and wrinkled—and greedy. Instead of trying my sign language on her I just held out a handful of coins. It was all the Austrian money I had left after paying for a carriage ride earlier. I expected her to take the ones she needed. She took them all. Talk about being left without a shilling!

Not too long ago I was watching the *Sound of Music,* which was filmed in Salzburg. Part of it was filmed in the square where I had sat and people-watched that day. All of a sudden to my surprise—I spied that same expensive little W.C.!

When Is Garbage Not Garbage?

One answer to that question is, "When you live in Australia." While I was there my friend spoke of the rubbish collector—not garbage collector. I think I like their term better. Doesn't sound so yukky.

Garbage is not garbage—or even rubbish—when it is a sack of clean glass jars and bottles, along with clean flattened tin cans. Then it becomes recycling material for my young ecology-minded neighbor. I hide big grocery bags of them in my broom closet for him to take to the recycling center.

I use my hall closet as a surplus supply closet. It holds all the bargains I can't resist. At last count I had eight rolls of paper towels. My neighbor said it looked like a soup kitchen one day when I opened the door. I like soup, and I save the labels for a friend who gives them to a charitable institution. I also save empty orange juice cans of a certain brand for her.

I save plastic cottage cheese and margarine containers for the church kitchen. We use these to take home goodies from pot lucks when the ladies start swapping leftovers. I save my empty yogurt and cottage cheese cartons for the Senior Nutrition Center where I sometimes eat when I'm not lunching out with friends. It is nearby and provides an easy way out of cooking and washing dishes. We use the containers there as doggie bags when we can't eat all our meal.

Clean plastic bags aren't garbage. I find a use for any size. Even bread wrappers are usable. I've known friends who crochet mats and even hats from them. But I just use mine for potato peelings and other "garbagey" trash.

Of course, every housewife saves all the rubber bands and twisties that come on bread and such. Once I even made a cross-shaped bookmark out of the flat plastic tabs from one kind of bread. I threaded ribbon through them somehow.

Can you throw away boxes? I mean greeting card boxes, shoe boxes, any pretty little box? I can't. When I get too many I unload them on a friend of mine who teaches. She finds lots of uses for them. I also give her the shells, rocks, and pictures that I save for a time and then don't know what to do with.

"One man's trash is another man's treasure."

I haven't even mentioned all the ways some housewives use leftover food instead of grinding it up in the garbage disposal. When our Work and Witness team from the church was at the European Nazarene Bible College the students set aside each Friday for missions. Lunch that day was soup and prayer. The money saved on lunch is given to missions. They also had a mission emphasis program during the lunch hour. We could sense their deep interest and compassion for those in third world countries. During table grace we prayed for the hungry of the world.

But to get back to the soup. It was made from leftovers of all the weekly meals. Iris, a young German girl, was their cook. She used her cooking skills to make, from a combination of foods that would never have occurred to me, the most delicious soup I have ever tasted. When I saw it being prepared in the kitchen I thought perhaps I should pray for myself as well as missions. But when it was served, along with generous slices of bread and butter, I ate two big bowls of it.

I only stopped to keep from looking like a pig. Iris's soup ladle must have had the powers of a magic wand.

I don't cook enough now to have many leftovers. But once in awhile enough accumulates in the refrigerator so that I can mix them all together. I call it "garbage soup." Doesn't sound good. Doesn't always look good. But it tastes great!

Here Comes the Dreamer

"And God spoke to him in a dream..." This statement is found often in the Old Testament before there was written scripture.

Very few of my dreams even make sense. And none could possibly be construed to give spiritual direction to me. All my life I've had recurring dreams of floating or skimming instead of walking. But I haven't taken this as a literal command. In my dreams I skim down stairways just above the steps. (But not on an escalator!) The closest I've come to floating down a staircase in real life was *falling* instead of walking.

Most of us have dreamed of being in a crowd (usually at church) when we are suddenly conscious of the fact that we are the only one standing there, like the emperor in his new suit. No one else seems to notice, but we are covered with embarrassment— and nothing else.

Almost all of my dreams are a complete jumble as though everything in them had been stirred by a giant eggbeater. So I am very content to rely for guidance upon the written Word of God and the still small voice of His Spirit within my heart.

> *There is a naughty little sprite*
> *Who jumbles up my dreams at night—*

As soon as I have gone to sleep
He piles them all up in a heap,
And then he stirs them 'round about
Until he knows beyond a doubt
That, from the start to the conclusion,
All will be complete confusion;
For though I try with all my might
They seldom ever turn out right.
No matter where, or what the season,
My dreams have neither rhyme nor reason.

They pay no heed to times or place—
Their mixed-up plots are a disgrace.
I wish this pesky little sprite
Would keep hands off my dreams at night.
If I ever catch the little gnome,
I'll box his ears and send him home!

Jinx?

Everyone hates my birthday. The mere mention of it brings a groan from my listeners. In fact, I'm sure I must have the most detested, feared, and despised birthday on the calendar. Although many people mark it as a day to be observed and much preparation is made for it—much of it is done grudgingly.

My birthday causes working women to panic, businessmen tremble, tycoons turn pale, and strong men cry—while bleary-eyed accountants work far, far into the night.

April 15. Many people participate in the day's activities, but few enjoy it.

And my last name is Pitts.

Can you think of a weirder combination? It is enough to jinx the strongest-hearted person. It wasn't always that way. For years the income tax deadline was March 15, until someone decided to louse up my birthday. I get my tax return sent in ahead of time. I don't intend to ruin a perfectly good birthday.

And I wasn't born with Pitts as my surname. I am "the Pitts" by choice. My life was a bowl of cherries, but all I wanted was the Pitts. I don't believe in such a thing as a jinx. Still—considering my birthdate and my surname—I'm glad it was my sister, Ruth, who was the 13th child born into our family instead of me. I already have two strikes against me. One more and I'd be out!

The last time I was at the beach with Ruth and her husband I decided to go for a walk. It was raining, and I love to walk on the beach by myself in the rain. When I tired of walking I leaned against a big, comfortable log to watch the waves. I had such a beautiful afternoon.

When I returned to the motel I took off my coat. It was then I discovered that the whole front of my slacks, from the waist to the knees, were covered with sticky, gummy pitch. Fortunately my coat had been unbuttoned so that it and my blouse stayed clean. That's typical! Out of all the hundreds of logs piled up on that beach, I picked a pitchy one to lean against.

I either have too many feet (though I'd hate to try doing with less) or else I don't pay attention to where I'm going. A group from one of the senior centers went to the coast for a day's outing. The rain had cleared, but there was still some water standing in places.

Four of us were strolling along when I stubbed my toe on a rock that was barely sticking above the sand. Before the others could blink their eyes I was flat on my stomach in a water puddle. I was up again almost that quick. One of them said he'd never seen anyone fall down and get up again so fast in his life.

The front of my blouse and slacks were soggy with wet sand. When we got back to where the others were I wiped it off the best I could with paper towels. Soon it had dried—polyester dries quickly—and after I brushed off the dry sand it looked as clean as new.

Some people don't care for polyester materials. But, with my propensity for mishaps, I dote on it. One evening three of us went out for pizza. Another habit of mine is that I can't talk without using my hands. That time I flung my hand out, knocking over a large glass of root beer. The whole thing spilled right into my lap. I had on a polyester dress that time. I grabbed the hem of it to keep the liquid from going all over the floor. My dress held that lap full of root beer just like a basin. None of it spilled. We sopped it up with all the paper napkins we could grab and a towel the waitress brought. By the time we left, my dress was dry and not even stained. If anyone should ask me the name of my best friend, I'd have to say—Polly Esther.

Another time we were at a different pizza place. I think my friends pick a different place each time because they get so embarrassed. I don't. I've been through it so many times—what's the use?

That same evening we had eaten upstairs and as we were coming down, I walked slowly and carefully.

"I'm really careful about steps anymore," I said to the friend beside me.

I looked up at her as I spoke and missed the bottom step! Kerplop—I belly-flopped out into the room, frightening the customers and almost colliding with a waiter carrying a loaded tray. I wasn't hurt. Three of my calloused friends walked on as if I didn't belong to them while the fourth one and the waiter helped me up.

I've been very fortunate in my falls. But if my stomach had bones in it, they'd have all been crushed long ago.

The craziest fall I ever had happened after church one Sunday morning while walking with friends to their car. I was yakking away and not watching my step. I stubbed both toes on a slight rise in the sidewalk and fell head-first into a holly bush in the adjoining yard. Of all the dumb things to do. It was also very humbling. I'm sure that I will never be conceited. How could a person possibly be conceited with her head stuck in a holly bush?

I'm a Coupon Clipper

No—not the kind associated with investments. I watch for the kind I can use at a grocery store—"cents off" coupons they are called. You've all seen them, and perhaps most of you toss them aside wishing your Sunday newspaper wasn't all cluttered up with the stupid things. That is the way I felt for years. I'm still an amateur at the game. And I intend to stay that way. I could never get as involved as some of my friends. But they are younger and have families. So I don't blame them for putting in the extra time and work on them.

In case you are a nonclipper, the sales pages feature savings for that week. You probably use those and the store coupons that are with them. But the ones that come in the "slicks" are pages of manufacturers' coupons. The nicest thing about these is that if you redeem them at a store that gives double coupons you get to save twice as much. Some say "no expiration date." Those are the best. Others have expiration dates, so you need to use them before a certain time.

There are also applications for rebates on some articles. These are sometimes in the store and often in the newspaper with the Sunday coupons. By filling out the blanks and enclosing all the things they ask for (after buying the article, of course) you get refunds from the company. Sometimes this is cash—sometimes more coupons.

I've cleared all these hurdles a few times and received rebates. But I was embarrassed when I put one in the mailbox addressed to "Free Soup and Crackers." I half-expected the postman to leave a crust of bread in my box the next day.

In order to send that one in I ate canned vegetable soup for a week so I could have the labels to send in, along with the proof of purchase from a box of crackers. Do you know what my refund will be? A coupon entitling me to three free cans of vegetable soup! Fortunately it takes at least six weeks for a delivery, and I won't have to use it right away. Perhaps by then I'll be able to look at a can of vegetable soup without turning green.

I wish the manufacturers and middlemen would reduce prices and forget about the coupons. But until they do I will go on playing their little game of "clip and save." The only way I can handle it is to go through the sale ads for the store where I shop, pick out the bargains, and then make out my list.

Then I sort out the coupons I can use on the sale items and put them with my list. If I go without a list and start rummaging around through my coupons, I get very frustrated. On one such day while I was fumbling around in a fistful of coupons, dropping one here and there, I remarked to a total stranger who walked past, "Some windy day I am going to take the whole bunch outside and watch them go *whoosh.*"

People Are My Hobby

We hear a lot about the "beautiful" people in the world—those whose main pursuits seem to be money and pleasure. One night after I had gone to bed I lay there thinking of all my wonderful friends. God has given me so many.

"Lord," I said with tears in my eyes, "I know who the beautiful people *really* are. They are my friends."

At times I have looked in the mirror and said to God, "I just can't see why people love me." Then I'd add quickly, "But don't tell me. I might spoil it if I knew."

I must have thought I had some hidden charm that they saw, but I couldn't. I was afraid if I found out what it was I might overdo it and spoil it all. (Dumb, huh?)

That night I again said, "Lord, I just can't see why . . ."

Before I got any further I distinctly heard Him say (and I could *feel* Him smile indulgently), "I'll tell you why. You don't have to worry about any hidden charms. The reason you have so many friends is because *I know you need them.*"

I laughed and cried at the same time . . . laughing at my foolish self and weeping with praise to a loving Father who knows I need friends and supplies so abundantly.

I have friends living next door and some in countries that before had been only shapes on a map or vague recollections of grade school geography lessons.

When I received a letter from a reader in Tasmania, I looked for it all over the continent of Africa and its surrounding islands. Then I noticed an Australian stamp on the letter and that gave me a clue! Since it is a small island below the Australian mainland, I guess you could say it is "down under down under."

I'm ashamed to admit (but I will anyway) that, after racking my brain, all I could recall about Tasmania was the term *Tasmanian devil*. I thought it was something like a whirling dervish. (Don't ask me what *that* is—or where. I simply do not know.) But I do know, now, what a Tasmanian devil is. I have a picture of one in my big AUSTRALIA book.

I keep telling my friends that a person doesn't have to be smart to write the kind of books I write. Perhaps now they will believe me.

* * *

I have friends whom I see often and some whom I have never seen. About 10 years ago I spent a month vacationing on the Oregon coast. Before I went, someone asked me if I had friends there.

"Oh, yes," I answered. "I just haven't met them yet."

I didn't realize at the time how many people would be described that way—among the residents and among the other vacationers who came and went. People in the church and in the little town urged me to move there.

One tiny cafe was my favorite eating place mainly because they cooked me such good breakfasts at noon. The egg whites had crispy brown ruffled edges—just the way I like them. During lunch one day I heard people congratulating the waitress on her birthday. I asked one of them her name, and before I left I folded a one dollar bill (more than my usual tip) in the white paper table napkin. On it I sketched some flowers with my pen and printed "Happy Birthday, Mary Lou." She was pleased at the little surprise.

I went there again on my last day in town. She was extra busy with more than the usual number of customers. There were two or three booths, and I was in one. All the others, mostly men, sat at the counter. As soon as one left at least one more came in.

She rushed past, apologizing for not getting to me. I told her I wasn't in any hurry at all and for her to serve all the others first. When everyone else was gone, she could get my order.

I sat for some time indulging in my favorite occupation of people-watching the customers, until there was finally no one left in the cafe except the waitress and me. She expressed appreciation for my patience, but I told her that I hadn't minded at all.

"Besides," I said, "I have to go home in the morning. So I wanted to leave a good impression on my last day in town."

She served my usual yummy breakfast, and we chatted as I ate. When I opened my wallet to pay as I was leaving, she wouldn't accept any payment.

"This is a going-away present because we have enjoyed you so much while you were here," was her explanation.

Where but in Yachats, Oreg., could that happen?

* * *

I have many churchgoing friends, and I have some behind prison bars on death row.

My grandson there—who is now a wonderful Christian—shares my books and my letters with them and relays messages between us. One man after reading *Let Me Keep Laughter* said, "I've never seen your grandmother, but I already love her."

I have the feeling that a frightened little boy is hiding inside each one of those men who have committed the crimes that brought them there. We cannot condone their deeds, but God can forgive their sins.

For that I am praying.

*   *   *

I have tall friends, short friends, and those in between. (Although the average height among my young friends is getting taller all the time. They regard me as a Pygmy.) I have skinny friends, stocky friends, paunchy friends, and some who (like me) are a bit unpleasingly plump.

I have some very young friends and one next door who is old enough to be my mother. And, of course, all ages in between, including some who won't tell their age.

I have friends with long noses, some with pug noses, and a lot who have just ordinary noses. I have friends with snow white hair, some with red hair, some brown, some blonde, and some who only their hairdresser knows for sure. I have friends with long hair, some with short hair, and some who can comb their hair with a washcloth.

I have handsome friends and pretty friends and a lot of friends who don't quite fit in either of those two categories. But they are all beautiful!

As long as I have people to love and who love me, the music will never stop playing.

HIDDEN BEAUTY

I thought her plain
Until she looked at
Me—and I saw stars
Shine in her eyes.

*I judged him stern
Until he smiled his
Sweet, heartwarming
Smile at me.*

*I would have called
Him dull had I
Not heard him read
A poem in a voice
As rich as deep-piled
Dark velvet.*

*I'm sure there is
In everyone some
Bit of hidden beauty—
Not seen by all, but
Placed there by
The hand of God.*

Some Mornings Are like That

Mornings are hard for me. Some are just plain traumatic. Twenty-five years of my husband working the night shift, and an inborn aversion to getting up in the morning, have made an owl of me. Let the larks have the morning—I'll take the nights.

As I'm writing this it is 3 A.M. I tried to be a normal person. I went to bed at a reasonable time and slept an hour or so. But why lie there wide awake most of the rest of the night when there is something I'd much rather do?

My best sleep (I don't care what the experts say) is from about 6 A.M. until 10 A.M. I set my snooze alarm on Saturday nights and on Sunday mornings it starts cheep, cheep, cheeping at me like a chicken in distress. I rouse enough to touch the thingamajig to hush it for another few minutes. After three or four sessions of this, I drag myself out of bed. My neighbor in the adjoining apartment is no doubt awake by now also. Some mornings I almost feel as if I were crawling out of my grave instead of my bed—all by myself—with none of the supernatural help I expect at the Rapture.

On one such morning I propelled myself the half block or so to church. (If I lived any farther, I'd never make it.)

Before I left home I checked myself in the full-length mirror. It's a good thing I did. My dress was on backward! I switched it right side to and left. One of the greeters opened the door for me and as I entered he lifted the cape from my shoulders saying, "Audre, do you really want to wear this wrong side out?" and changed it for me.

At the beginning of Sunday School class the man behind me handed me a basket. Without looking I dropped in a $1.00 bill and handed it back. At least I tried to hand it back, but he wouldn't take it. He finally convinced me it wasn't the offering basket. Each month the publicity chairman of our missionary group makes clever little announcements. These are passed around in our class the Sunday before our meeting. That was what he was trying to give me.

Roger, our teacher, saw what had happened and started chuckling. Finally, he couldn't keep quiet. "Most of you get these announcements for nothing," he said, "but Audre paid a dollar for hers."

You'd have thought that was enough for one morning—but not quite. Later in the lesson Roger asked me to read some scripture from our lesson quarterly.

"No," I explained resignedly, "but I'll read it from my Bible. I seem to have picked up my *Come Ye Apart* (our church devotional magazine) this morning when I left instead of my quarterly."

The Age of Wrinkles

Sitting in Wednesday evening prayer meeting recently, I casually looked down at the back of my left hand. There, outlined by brown age spots, is an almost perfect replica of the Little Dipper. If I'd look more closely, I might even find the North Star. At the rate the spots are increasing I may soon have the entire Milky Way.

This business of aging is a peculiar thing. It takes over gradually, beginning at birth, and continues until we die. Yet we don't think of it as beginning until we reach a certain time in life—the age of wrinkles, gray hair, and brown spots.

One of the strangest things about it is that it is only the outside of us that seems to grow older. In my heart I'm still young. I still like pizza and tacos. I like to laugh just as much as I ever did. But I can't seem to get the message across to my body that I'm still young.

Sea creatures outgrow their shells and get new ones. We only outgrow our clothes. Snakes shed their skins for new ones. We have to keep the same skin we've exposed to sun, wind, and saltwater for years. Then it surprises us when we look in the mirror and find lines and wrinkles. I'm not sure just what is the difference between a line and a wrinkle. I've decided that lines are probably just wrinkles that we don't want to admit having. My daughter used to call the crow's-feet around my eyes "laughing wrinkles."

When I am tempted to bemoan the lines in my face I suddenly remember the most beautiful face in the world—that of Mother Teresa. She doesn't waste *her* time standing in front of the mirror worrying about wrinkles. She's out there giving her very life to help the sick and dying ones. Her beautiful wrinkles are furrows worn by the tears of compassion that she sheds for those to whom she constantly ministers.

God bless you, Mother Teresa.

* * *

When I was eight years old our family went to a neighbor's home for a church meeting. The lady who was in charge had snow white hair and a couple of gold teeth. I thought she was the most beautiful person I had ever seen. When we got home I told my folks that when I got old I wanted white hair and *all* gold teeth.

I had to wait until I was 60 for my hair to start graying, and it will never be snow white unless I bleach it. I may have to be content with tattle-tale gray and one gold crown on my tooth.

I have one other option. I've joined the rank of elderly ladies whose pink scalps show through their thinning hair when they sit in front of you at church. Maybe I'll just buy a snow white wig!

I won't mind being bewigged, bespectacled, bespotted, and wrinkled, with a crippled knee—as long as the music keeps on playing in my heart.

STOWAWAY

There is a little
Stowaway hiding
Somewhere inside
Of me—sometimes

*In my heart, still
Mourning her broken
Doll at age five.*

*She loves to play
In my memory-box
And can amuse herself
For hours, sorting out
Souvenirs of half-
Forgotten happenings.
And then she creeps
Into my mind, chuckling
Over Alice in Wonderland
Which she keeps on my
Bookshelf—or getting
All excited about a
Colored leaf—or a
Butterfly—and you
Wouldn't believe her
Fantasies—(I'm glad
I don't believe them!)*

*At other times she's
In my stomach—
Teasing for ice cream
Cones and cotton candy.
Perhaps you've guessed
That my stowaway
Is the little girl I
Used to be—I've
Never had the heart
To tell her she must
Leave—besides, to
Tell the truth, I don't
Really want her to!*

2 Chronicles 20:21

Our pastor frequently talks to us about the power of praise. One of his sermon texts was 2 Chron. 20:21, ". . . he [Jehoshaphat] appointed singers unto the Lord, and that should praise the beauty of holiness, as they went out before the army" (KJV).

The NIV translation reads, "as they went out at the *head* of the army . . ."

Right there on the front line—not the mightiest warriors, not the sturdiest chariots of warfare, not the brave soldiers with gleaming shields and flashing swords. No! the choir! And that was in real hand-to-hand battle. They weren't just playing games.

I'd read that verse many times. Perhaps I should say my eyes had skimmed over it many times. But I hadn't really thought about it. As Pastor Daryl spoke that morning I had a sneaking hunch that if any choir I was involved in was ever ordered to the front lines of a battle, I'd retire posthaste.

I've been trying to retire from our church choir for six years. I even wrote a poem to that effect and gave it to our director:

This old voice is gettin' squeaky
And the notes are gettin' higher;

These old joints are gettin' creaky
  And I'm ready to retire.
Can't get up on Sunday morning
  For the practice I require—
Ain't gonna sing with you much longer,
  I'm gettin' ready to leave the choir.
Ain't gonna need my worn black folder,
  Ain't gonna need my robe much more—
I'll just hang it on its hanger
  And go walkin' out the door.
Ain't gonna write no crazy poems—
  My poor brain is gettin' tired.
Ain't gonna heckle you much longer—
  I'm gettin' ready to leave the choir.

The reference to the crazy poems was about the ones I was always asked to write for our choir parties. About the heckling—well, maybe I *did* give him a *few* problems.

But he only laughed and said he knew I wouldn't quit. And I didn't. I've retired at least once annually since then. I really enjoy singing and making melody. (Maybe we'd better scratch that out about the melody.) Besides, I love all the other choir members and like to be with them. But this time I've really retired—I think.

Even when I'm not in the choir I sit as far up front as possible during services. And my heart sings along with them as they sing. After so many years of watching the director's hands, I have become programmed. A few times I have almost stood in the congregation when he motioned for the choir to stand.

But if in the choir or out of the choir—my heart will go on singing. And the music will never stop playing—e'en down to old age!

The Confessions of a Collector

We human beings love to collect. If a person wanted to spend his life in research, he could fill an encyclopedia with information about collectors and their collections. A Japanese insurance company very recently paid more than $39 million for a Van Gogh painting of sunflowers to add to their art collection.

When I heard of that I felt better about the modest amount of money I've spent on my music boxes. My advice to one and all is that if you don't want to get started on a collection, never acquire more than *one* of anything (except shoes and socks, of course, and things of a practical nature). Because when you get the second one you've already started a collection, and the urge to add to it keeps growing.

I speak from experience. When I was in the fifth grade a boy in my class brought a photograph album to show. (That was years before they started calling it "Show and Tell.") When the album was opened it played a tune. That was the day I fell in love—not with the boy, but with his music box. It was the first one I'd ever seen.

I've carried that love in my heart ever since and was a grandmother when I received my first music box. I had decided that I wanted only one, and I would be completely satisfied. One Christmas my husband gave me a pink bone china teapot. When lifted to pour, it played an appropriate tune. I was content. At last I had a music box.

But the following Christmas our daughter gave me a musical powder box. Then I had a collection! From then on the list kept growing. My family always knew what to buy me for Christmas or birthdays—another music box.

After my daughter and husband were gone I kept adding to my collection. I'd buy them as souvenirs of places I visited. One year I said, "No more music boxes. I'm being crowded out. I'm not buying any more."

That Christmas I received five music boxes from friends. So I threw up my hands, opened my purse, and kept right on. I've "definitely quit" buying several times since. Then I see one that is altogether different from any I have. I love every one. Whenever I go into a gift shop I am as lured to the music box display as a child is to the candy case. I follow the tinkling sound of their music the way the children followed the Pied Piper of Hamelin.

I saw one in Switzerland that was priced at $5,000. That is probably a hundred times more than I paid for my whole collection over a 40-year period. I bought some in Switzerland and Germany, but for a much lower price.

I enjoy my little musical toys, but I know that when I am gone a lot of my treasures may become someone else's trash. That's OK. I'll just enjoy their music as long as I live and then trade them in for a harp!

Things That Go Bump in the Night

On one of our vacations at the beach we stayed in a two-story cottage. I slept in the downstairs bedroom, and Ruth and Don slept upstairs. Sometime during the night I was awakened by rustling, scratching noises in my room. I hastily turned on the light and glanced around but could see nothing. I snapped off the bed lamp and lay back down; but the noises persisted. Were they coming from under my bed?

By that time I was in the clutches of terror. On occasions my active imagination ceases to be my friend. Tonight it had turned on me with a vengeance. I got up on all fours and hung my head over the edge of the bed as far as I could to see if there really was something crawling around under there. It's amazing I didn't fall on my head. But I wouldn't get *out* of bed for fear something might grab my bare toes. Rising up I looked across the room and peered under the dresser. But I couldn't see a thing.

This time I kept the light on. I couldn't stand being alone in the dark with creepy-crawlies. It wasn't a constant sound, so I would doze off only to wake with a jerk at a new onslaught of noises. I was unusually tired from walking on the beach that day. I was too sleepy to stay awake and too frightened to sleep. In this half-awake, half-asleep state of limbo I imagined all sorts of things.

By now I even had a visual image of the creatures, though I hadn't seen any. In my mind they were scaly with crablike claws. I was sure I could hear their claws scratching the floor under the dresser. And sometimes it sounded as if they were on the wall right above my head.

After what seemed a long time, I heard footsteps descending the stairs and was sure it was my sister. Help was near! It turned out to be Don, but I rushed out blubbering, "Oh, Don, I'm so scared!"

He sleepily assured me that nothing was wrong and went on to the bathroom. Fortified by the knowledge that another human being was within call, I screwed up my courage and looked under the bed, the dresser, above my bed, and in every corner of the room. After that I turned out the light and slept.

The next morning Ruth said she had heard seagulls landing on the roof and walking around all night. That, no doubt, was the scratching I had heard above my bed—the sound of their talons traveling down the wall.

Don went outside and came back to report that he had solved the mystery of the scratching under the dresser. There were signs of someone's dog having dug in the flower beds during the night. The rattle of the dead leaves and big flower heads rustling and bumping against the outside wall were my creatures who scratched with their crablike claws.

I hope I never let my imagination run away with me like that again! With fervency I echo the old Cornish prayer,

> *From ghoulies and ghosties*
> *And long-leggity beasties*
> *And things that go bump in the night,*
> *Dear Lord, deliver us.*

And to that list I would also add "scratchety creatures with crablike claws."

I'm Not the Only One

I've learned that I'm not the only one who does dumb things. My husband worked three different shifts a week, on a rotating basis. One day I found him sitting on the side of the bed, with one sock on his foot and the other in his hand, looking very bewildered. Sheepishly, he turned to me and said, "Am I getting up or going to bed?"

He couldn't figure out if he should put on the sock he was holding and go to work or take the one off his foot and go to bed. I wasn't quick-witted enough to tell him to smell the sock he was holding to find out. I just told him he was supposed to go to bed. He was so tired he just couldn't remember.

* * *

My friend Gracie had just bought a pair of electric scissors and was anxious to try them out. She laid a piece of dress material on the bed and a pattern on that—because it was a handy place to work. She was delighted with the way they worked and zipped merrily along. Picking up the cut-out dress she saw, with horror-filled eyes, that she had cut too deep. There was her beautiful bedspread with a hole in it the size and shape of her dress pattern.

That's the same Gracie who cooked up a big pot of chili and invited her family over to help eat it. After the first bite neither they—nor she—wanted any part of it. She had mistakenly used cinnamon in it instead of chili powder.

* * *

The Beaverton, Oreg., SAM group had invited me to speak at one of their meetings. The next morning before I left for the bus station a neighbor came rushing to the home where I had stayed overnight. She had bought the book *I Talk to Myself a Lot* the night before.

"I read it through before I went to sleep," she said, "and I just had to tell you about the time I lost my lower dentures."

She had looked everywhere with no success so had to get new ones. Six months later, while spring cleaning, she found them down inside the wire coils in the bedsprings (the old-fashioned springs that a lot of you may not have ever seen—but I remember them well). She said she must have taken them out and put them under her pillow while reading in bed. From there they had slipped down and fallen into the bedsprings.

* * *

We have a favorite restaurant where we go in Depoe Bay when my sister and her husband come to Oregon. One morning we stopped there for our "second breakfast." We had a booth by the window where the sun was streaming in. The base for holding a coffee carafe was on the table, but the waitress hadn't yet brought coffee. The sunlight was glinting off the chrome top of it right in Don's eyes. So he very cleverly covered it up with a paper napkin. Ruth and I were complimenting him on his ingenuity when a waitress came dashing over and snatched it off. There was a lighted candle in that thing! We saw the candle but the sunlight was so bright the flame didn't show up. In another second or so the napkin would have caught fire. The waitress grinned and shook her head at Don.

"You're a little fire-bug, aren't you?" she said.

Ruth and I still tease him about being a little fire-bug.

* * *

I must tell you about Kathleen. She was planning to go on a trip with George and Anne in their motorhome. She loaded all her clothes into her car and drove to their place. The front door was open, so she walked in with her clothes on hangers, slung over her shoulder.

"You hoo," she called, "I'm here."

A man she had never seen before walked into the room and asked who she was looking for.

She was so rattled that all she could say was, "Uh-oh—I was looking for George."

She said she couldn't even think of Anne's name, she was so flustered.

"George who?" the man persisted.

And then, in her agitated frame of mind, she couldn't think of their *last* name. So she just said, "Oh, forget it," and made a hasty exit.

She drove one more block down the street and found the right house.

* * *

Kathleen is also the one who moved from one address to another while her husband was at work. She wanted to live close to town, but he liked it out where they were.

She picked out a house in town and contacted a moving company. She told them the exact time to arrive—after her husband had gone to work. When he got home she was gone and so was everything else. He opened the door and wondered if he was losing his mind. Then a neighbor, with whom Kathleen had thoughtfully left a message, told him where his new home was.

Acting with wifely wisdom, she invited company for dinner, to give him a cooling-off period.

* * *

Then there's my friend who lives in a distant state. She and her husband had an upstairs apartment with several flights of steps to climb, so she tried to make her trips up and down the stairs count.

She lives at a pell-mell pace, full-speed ahead. One morning she was in her usual rush but thought she had everything well organized before leaving the apartment. She had her husband's suit on a hanger, to leave at the cleaners, and a plastic bag full of garbage to deposit on the way to the car.

Snatching up her purse along with the suit and the bag of garbage, she paused an instant at the door to ask God to keep her calm through the day. Then she raced down the steps, opened the garbage can and left her deposit as she ran past and then on to the car. As she opened the car door, she realized she was still carrying the plastic bag. She had put her husband's suit in the garbage!

"Lord," she wailed as she went back to retrieve the suit which, by then, really did need to go to the cleaners, "I *asked* You to keep me *calm*."

I Like Rain

It's a good thing I do since I live in western Oregon where we get plenty of it. I often tell people that we moved here because of the rain. Having gone through drought and dust-bowl days of the 1930s we craved rain.

After leaving the Midwest we lived in the mountains of California for six years. After shoveling his way in and out of the driveway every day for months of every year, my husband decided to swap the snow for rain. He said that at least he wouldn't have to shovel the rain.

Of course, I like sunshine, too, but rain is special. I like to walk in the rain—even in a downpour if I'm equipped. Sometimes I'm *not* equipped.

Rain on the roof has such a cozy sound. One day when our winter rains had extended into June and everyone was exasperated, it started raining again. I looked up from my desk and out of the window. I could feel my muscles relaxing. "I don't care what they say, God," I said, "I *still* like rain."

Having thus assured the Almighty of my approval, I moved over to my rocker and watched the raindrops fall.

> *Soft patter of the*
> *Rain upon my roof,*
> *The ticking of the clock,*
> *And a kitten's purr,*

*The crackling of a wood fire
On the hearth and
The gentle hissing
Of the kettle as
It sings while
Heating water
For my tea—
Sounds of contentment
On a rainy day—
Sounds that make
My heart croon
Its own contented melody.*

Number One Chicken

After Easter a few years ago our pastor requested volunteers to do some follow-up calls on the visitors. Even though I'm the No. 1 chicken when it comes to knocking on doors, I decided to make another try at it.

I must not have been the only chicken in the congregation because there were very few who responded besides the regulars. We were to meet at the church and when I got there I found mostly man-and-wife teams. I was alone and Ed's wife didn't come, so they made us a team.

The leader gave us some cards with names and addresses of people we didn't know. But we started out bravely enough.

"Since this first card has a lady's name on it, I will do the greeting and then introduce you," I said.

He agreed. So far, so good. We arrived at the first house. A light was showing in the kitchen but not in the living room. I rang the bell—that is about the hardest part for me. I began weakening when I had to ring it the second time. A lady came to the door without turning on a light in the room. In the semidarkness we could see that she had been crying.

I panicked completely. I couldn't think of her name or my name or the name of our church. And when I tried to introduce Ed I couldn't think of his name. I sputtered and stammered and managed to ask if we had come at an inconvenient time. She said, "Yes," so I apologized (in fear and trembling) and said we'd come another time. Then I sent up a silent prayer for forgiveness. Someone else might go, but *I* knew I never could. I was already a basket case.

It was a stormy night and the rain pelted us on our way to the car. Just as we got in, a bolt of lightning split the sky, followed by a tremendous clap of thunder. That wasn't too good for my shattered nerves either.

As Ed drove on to the next house I told him it was all his from now on. If he would knock and break the ice—then I could do some of the talking. We didn't have any more success there. They were having a late dinner. Ed made the apologies this time and we left. Then we both threw in the towel.

Ed does a lot of hospital visitation among our members. So, while the rains descended and the lightning flashed and the thunder rolled, he drove to the hospital. We visited several of our people there and enjoyed doing it. They were very glad to see us.

Some people really enjoy calling—even cold turkey. Every time I've tried it I was the cold turkey!

Years ago my sister and I went to call on some of the absentees from my Sunday School class. There were *two* chickens that day. The first place we went, we knocked on the door and then, as our courage ebbed, we *sneaked* off the porch before she could get to the door.

We hear a lot about the gifting of the Spirit and finding out what our gift is. I know definitely what mine is *not!*

Bowl 'em Over!

A couple of years ago I agreed to be the chairman of a church fellowship group. One evening we decided to go bowling, then to a restaurant afterward. There were 10 of us on this occasion. Some in the bunch were good bowlers. And then there was me.

In my youth bowling alleys were off limits. Now, of course, bowling is a recreation in which the whole family can share. They don't even call them "alleys" any more. They are lanes. I'd never been on a bowling floor, worn a pair of bowling shoes, or even tried to lift a bowling ball. I had no idea they were so heavy! They got me the lightest ball in the place, but it still felt like it weighed a long ton.

We divided into two teams and the fun began. I'm sure I broke the world record for throwing the most gutter balls in one evening. My serves (is that what you call them?) had so little power behind them that the balls rolled slowly, slowly, and more slowly. Then most of them just rolled over in the gutter and died.

After I broke a fingernail (by not getting it out of the hole soon enough), I decided to put the ball down on the floor in front of me and *shove* it down the lane. Some of my team thought maybe I could do better that way. But I didn't. I made just as many gutter balls as ever.

When any of the others left some pins standing they groaned with frustration. Whenever I knocked even one pin down I shouted! My combined score for two games was less than 50, I think.

Anyway, we had a good time. Everyone said they'd never had so much fun bowling before. We all laughed until we cried. We were the only ones there at the time except the manager. He enjoyed it, too.

The next day I mailed each one in the group a copy of some doggerel I had written after I got home from the party.

AUDRE AT THE BOWLING ALLEY

Down to the bowling alley she went,
And over the bowling ball she bent:
Grasping the ball and taking aim
She gave it a shove and it rolled down the lane.
But all she could do was stand there and sputter
When 99 percent of them went in the gutter!

That was not only the first time I tried bowling. It was the last. But that isn't saying I might not try it again some day.

I Can't Blame It on Old Age

No matter what I do I can't rightfully use my advancing years as an alibi. I've spent my life—from my youth up—doing stupid things.

On one such occasion my husband and brother-in-law were boating on a small pond just outside of town. While they were out in the Curly-Q (our homemade boat which I named for my brother, Curly, who helped build it), Ruth and I went for a walk. It was after dark, but there was still enough light from the moon and stars so that we could see our way.

Suddenly a dog barked nearby. I thought we should just stand quietly so that he would be less apt to chase us. So, I said, "Don't run, Ruth. Don't run!"

Only I didn't exactly *say* it. I sort of yelled it back over my shoulder as I darted pell-mell up the road as though a whole pack of baying hounds were at my heels. I didn't intend to run. I didn't even know I *was* running for a while. My feet just took off on their own and it was awhile, before I could get them stopped.

I was only in my 20s then. So it couldn't have been senility. Ruth sat down in the road and collapsed with laughter.

I had a bone-chilling experience one night when Raymond was at work. I woke in the wee hours and reached for the chain to turn on the bed lamp. But instead of the chain I grabbed an ice-cold *hand* in the dark! Just before I died of fright I found the chain and switched on the light. It was my *own* hand I had grabbed. It was asleep and couldn't feel my touch. Neither did it have any feeling of being connected with the rest of my body.

* * *

Blue was Raymond's favorite color. Any dress I had was pretty as long as it was blue. He was the same way with his ties. One year, when red was especially popular for men, I tried to persuade him to buy one. It would have gone so nicely with his dark hair and eyes. He weakened enough to buy a *dark* red one. But then he didn't want to wear it. He may have worn it two or three times, but I think it was actually only once. He didn't like it at all. He kept right on wearing his beloved blue ones.

The day my niece came to get his clothes to take to the mortuary she asked which tie I wanted her to take. She worded it wrong. She should have asked which *he* would have wanted her to take.

I looked at all his blue ones hanging there on the rack—and then I handed her the dark red one.

I'm still wondering—was that part of my innate feminine desire to have the last word?

* * *

Our Sunday School class was having dinner at one of our favorite restaurants. It was one of those "all you can eat" places, and we all ate plenty. When I got to the groaning stage our young pastor began teasing me and asking if I wanted more food. He even offered to go get some for me. I protested vigorously—so, of course, he went.

I watched him as he was coming back and, just before he reached me, I slid out of my chair and under the table.

That was almost 20 years ago. I couldn't scoot that fast now.

* * *

Just before the beginning of Sunday School a friend whispered to me that the hem was out of my dress all across the back. There wasn't time to do anything about it then so I hurriedly sat down near the back. At the end of class I was asked to come to the front and read something.

"I'm sorry," I apologized, "I'll be glad to read it from here, but I was just informed that the hem of my dress is out in the back. And by the way," I added, "if any of you ladies happen to have some safety pins or a sewing kit with you, would you please come to my rescue when class is over?"

One dear lady had a string of them in her purse, which she carried for emergencies with her grandchildren. We retired to the ladies' room and the wayward hem was pinned back in place. It took all eight of her pins.

Since that time I, too, have carried a string of them in my purse. No one has ever needed all of them at one time—but I have been able to help others now and then with more minor emergencies.

* * *

One night I was reading my newspaper. I had been busy all day and that was the first I had looked at it. I noticed an item that told of a blizzard in Concordia, Kans. I thought if it made our Oregon newspaper it must be a pretty big one.

I looked at the clock. It was 9:30. My sister and her husband both worked, and I knew ten o'clock was their bedtime. But I figured I'd have time to catch them just before that. The phone rang a number of times and then my brother-in-law answered. I said, "Don, is it snowing there?"

He kind of laughed and said he hadn't looked outside for a while.

I said, "Is Ruth there?" I knew she would be.

He hemmed a bit and said, "Well, she's in bed."

"At 9:30?" I asked.

"Well, you know, it's almost midnight here," he answered.

I'd forgotten the two hours difference in time! Imagine getting called out of bed at midnight and being asked if it is snowing! Ruth came to the phone. I told her what I'd read, and she said the blizzard had been about a week before and it was fine there then. (The news to our paper must have come by pony express and the pony got stuck in a snowdrift.)

That has been a standing joke ever since. Every now and then when I'm talking with Ruth, Don will get on the extension and say, "Hello, Audre, is it snowing there?"

* * *

I have a small flashlight that I sometimes carry in my purse. One afternoon, just before a memorial service was to begin at the church, I was searching in my purse for some elusive object. Finally, I turned on the flashlight, shown it down into the depths of the purse, and found what I wanted. My friend, Muriel, who was sitting beside me almost strangled trying to control her amusement.

I told her I was still waiting for some enterprising inventor to come up with a purse with a light that turned on automatically when it was opened. If they can do it with refrigerators and ovens, why can't they do it with purses? It would save a lot of fumbling and mauling just to find a cough drop in church.

And while this hoped-for inventor is at it, he might add a trash compactor for all the gum wrappers, used tissues, and out-of-date church bulletins that seem to congregate there.

I am definitely *not* a Mrs. Fixit person around the house. Some women can do all sorts of things—even putting a new what-you-may-call-it on the end of an electric cord when it has gone kaput.

Not I. Once I quickly unplugged an electric clock and threw it away. I thought something terrible was wrong with it and didn't want it to catch fire or something. Weeks later it dawned on me that the alarm jigger had been accidentally pulled out. That was all. It was just the alarm going off. Well, it alarmed me all right. It also cost me the price of a new clock.

When we got our first TV set, it was the kind that had tubes in it. A book came with it that told how to figure out what had gone wrong whenever something did go wrong. It described, with illustrations, how the set acted and which tubes were responsible for it.

My husband was a Mr. Fixit. He could do anything. But I had more time to study the instruction book than he did. If something went wrong with the set while he was at work, I would look in the book and find out the cause. Then I chose the right tubes from a supply he kept in a cupboard drawer. When he came home I had all the tubes laid out on the dining room table and would tell him which ones to put where. We made a very successful team.

Now, of course, they don't have tubes. I've had my present small color set for about nine years. It worked perfectly for the first few years. Then it got so it didn't always respond when I would turn it on. The TV was very inconsistent. Sometimes it did and sometimes it didn't.

I intended to call a repairman. But one day by accident— no, it really *wasn't* an accident—I hit it on purpose. The picture came on clear and beautiful. So for over three years that's been my way of handling the situation. I probably should call a repairman. It may blow up in my face some time—just to get even.

I was amused while reading a book by the poet Martha Snell Nicholson. She said that as a child she often heard them sing in church,

> *Jesus, lover of my soul,*
> *Let me to thy bosom fly.*

She always wondered what a bosom fly was.

One Sunday evening in summer during choir practice an overgrown fly wandered in from outdoors and zoomed straight for Charlotte, who was seated beside me. She tried to brush it off with her music but, evidently lured by the fragrance of her perfume, it refused to leave.

"There's one," I whispered excitedly. *"There's* a bosom fly!"

I don't know what happened to the fly after that, but Charlotte and I didn't get much singing done for the rest of the rehearsal period.

Gweneth

One rainy day while riding the city bus I watched a young lady crossing the intersection. Her bare head was thrown back, and she was singing blithely as she made her way across with the aid of her white cane.

There was such an air of carefree abandon about her—such an expression of complete enjoyment of the rain.

She will never know the moment of joy she is giving me, I thought. But I knew I would never forget her. That night, at home, I wrote a poem about her.

Two or three years later I was sitting in a bus downtown. Shortly before the driver came to start his route, a girl appeared at the open door. She asked which bus it was. For a moment no one answered, not realizing that she could not see. She asked again.

This time I answered. She nodded, smiled, and climbed the steps.

"Here is a seat by me," I offered.

Her clear laugh rang out, "Here could mean anywhere to me," she said. "Could you tap the back of the seat, please?"

I tapped and she made her way confidently toward me. She was not wearing dark glasses, or glasses of any kind, and it was hard to recognize the fact of her blindness. We visited a mile a minute as the bus made its way along the route.

"You know," I told her, "two or three years ago I saw another blind girl crossing the Twenty-ninth Street intersection. She was singing and looked so happy as she walked in the rain. I've never forgotten her."

Again that laughter pealed out. (There is just no other word that describes her laughter but "peal.") "That was me," she said. "I do it all the time."

Then I was really interested. I told her I had written a poem about her. She was as delighted as a child who'd been given a lollipop. She wanted me to recite the poem to her. But all I could remember were the last few lines:

> *Rain in her face,*
> *Sunlight in her smile,*
> *And happiness*
> *An aura about her.*

She loved the way I had described her. We exchanged names, addresses, and telephone numbers. I gave her an extra deposit slip torn from my checkbook with mine on it, and I wrote hers down on the back of another one without tearing it out. We made promises to get together for lunch someday and when it was time for me to leave the bus, we parted with a hug.

Time slipped away at its usual fast pace, but a few weeks later I decided to call Gweneth to see if we could get together. I got my wallet and looked for her address that I had written on the back of a deposit slip in it. It wasn't there. I had used up all the checks—again at the usual fast pace—then thrown away the rest of it without remembering the address on the back. I was heartsick, frustrated, and very disgusted with myself. I remembered her first name but—try as I may—I could not think of the last. I tried for weeks, which ran into months, to no avail. I feared that I had lost her from my life after those two brief glimpses.

Months later my telephone rang. It was Gweneth!

"I've tried for months to call you," she said, "but you were never home. I had almost decided that you weren't really true—you were only a fantasy and I had never really met you."

We met for lunch at a downtown cafe. I have never known a person who seems more alive with the joy of living than Gweneth. She is a beautiful young woman of 32—but looks younger—with dark hair and hazel eyes. (She says they are green.) Only the overlarge pupils betray the fact that those eyes cannot see. And even when you know it you can scarcely believe it.

She has not always been blind, so she says she still reacts as a seeing person. She looked at me as directly as anyone with perfect vision whenever I was talking. I read the poem to her that day. She recorded it on her tape recorder, and I gave her a copy.

We chatted over our sandwiches at length and then went out into the sunshine. All that long sunny afternoon we sat on the steps of the mall fountain talking eagerly. We were anxious to find out as much as possible about each other. I discovered that music was a very important part of her life. She carries a small cassette recorder with her wherever she goes and often sings along with the tapes as she is walking. That is what she was doing the first day I saw her.

I got her name and address again and—would you believe it—I lost that one! I have no idea what I wrote it on that time but, whatever it was, I could not find it *anywhere*. And, as before, I couldn't remember her last name. I searched and racked my brain and then I prayed. One day it dawned on me that it was a two-part name and the first part was Van. So I got the telephone directory and started down the list of Vans. When I got to the Van F's, there it was. Gweneth VanFrank.

Now I have it written all over the place, and I shouldn't lose it again.

   When I had reached this point in my manuscript I laid down my pen and dialed Gweneth's telephone number. She was excited when I told her I was writing a "Gweneth" chapter in my book.

   We met the next week at the same place as before. I read what I had written, and she was pleased with it. Again, we visited away the hours. There will be other times and meetings, I'm sure. We both agree that our meeting on the bus was not just happenstance.

   This is the poem I wrote the first time I saw her singing in the rain:

> *I saw happiness today*
> *As I watched a*
> *Blind girl, singing as*
> *She made her way across*
> *A busy street—her*
> *Shining face uplifted*
> *To the falling rain*
> *And her white cane*
> *Tapping to the*
> *Rhythm of her song—*
>
> *Rain in her face,*
> *Sunlight in her smile,*
> *And happiness—an*
> *Aura about her.*

   God bless you, Gweneth. May heaven's richest blessings rest upon you. And, for you, may the music never stop playing.

I've Looked Everywhere!

I did it. I moved out of my cozy little studio apartment, where I had only one room to search for lost articles, into a two-bedroom next door. Now I can't find *anything*. I moved two years ago and found my camera just last week. I have my name in for the studio again if it is ever available. Until then I'll just have to be content to hold all-night search parties for lost articles.

My upstairs neighbor helped me with my moving. In fact, she did a lot more of it than I did. We decided this past winter that there was a method in her madness of moving me—though, of course, neither of us could have foreseen it at the time.

The week before Thanksgiving she had emergency heart surgery. I talked to her over the phone in her hospital room the day after her release from the intensive care unit. I told her if she wasn't able to manage the steps up to her apartment for awhile she could use the guest room in my downstairs apartment.

Three weeks after surgery she came. The day her friend brought her she looked like a little sick bird. I could hardly believe it—she was always so active and full of energy. I gave her a cup of warm broth, then put her to bed.

If there is one thing I am not, it is a nurse. My heart quailed within me as I faced the responsibility of caring for one so ill. She'd had a rough time of it. They thought they were losing her several times during surgery. And she still wasn't out of the woods. Maybe you think I didn't do some serious praying!

The only way the doctor would let her come so soon was with the promise that she would have someone with her 24 hours a day for the first week. Others of her friends came to "baby-sit" with her when I needed to be gone. Also, during that first week, I—who constantly warn friends *not* to phone before 10 A.M.—set my alarm at the unearthly hour of 6 A.M. so I could give her a pill. Then, at the sound of the alarm each morning, I would struggle out of bed, shuffle half-asleep to her bedside, waken her, and hand her the pill and glass of water I'd put on her nightstand before retiring the night before. Then I'd sleepwalk back to my own bed again.

She improved steadily—if slowly—and at the end of three weeks she was able to negotiate the steps and return to her own apartment.

We've talked since about the ease with which we adjusted to the situation. We are both quite independent but, in spite of her illness, we enjoyed the fellowship of being together. We missed it after she went home.

There were only two minor mishaps. One night I quietly got up and crept noiselessly to the bathroom without turning on a light—so as not to waken her. I didn't know she had done the same thing just moments before. I pushed the door back and cracked her on the head.

Another time we were in the kitchen. She was fixing her breakfast cereal, and I was putting away the sponge mop I'd used the night before. I'll never know how I managed to do it, but I somehow caught the tip of the handle under the nosepiece of her glasses and flipped them off. They didn't break, and fortunately I hadn't poked her in the eye with the mop handle. We had evidently turned at the same instant, not seeing the other. Had we practiced for hours, we could never have repeated the same trick.

In spite of my rough treatment, she has recovered. She told me one day that I had saved her life by taking her in. But I think she may have saved her own by leaving before I mutilated her in another freak accident.

I Like Apartment Living
—But

Those who live in apartment houses know that sounds can be deceiving. At one time I was sure that the young couple living above me practiced flamenco dancing. I could hear the rhythm and tapping of their feet. A few years and a few tenants later I found out that one of them was just using a typewriter on the dining table, which wasn't sitting level on the floor. As the person struck the keys, the table legs danced on my ceiling to the same rhythm.

Later, a young couple with a baby occupied that apartment. They had been there only a short time, and I had not really become acquainted with them. I didn't know where he worked or what his hours were.

One night the baby cried for a long time. I could hear a man's voice and a woman's voice. Then suddenly the woman screamed. At the same time it sounded as if a body was rolling across the floor. And the baby's cries became loud shrieks.

I was scared silly. Had someone broken in while the husband was at work to abuse the woman and baby? What should I do? Again, it sounded like a body thudding to the floor.

I grabbed the telephone by my bedside, and as quickly as my shaking fingers could, I dialed the police. I told them I didn't know if anything was really wrong, but I was afraid there was.

They came immediately. I heard the policeman talking upstairs. Then he tapped on my door. He told me not to be afraid and explained the situation. Young Jonah (the baby) wanted to spend the night in bed with his folks. Papa was trying to be a stern parent and make him sleep in his own bed.

And the body rolling across the floor? It seems that the young mother's nerves gave way. She was sitting at that same uneven table, and in a nervous frenzy she screamed and stamped her feet on the floor (my ceiling) and pounded rapidly on the table with her fists. And the table legs danced on my ceiling.

I felt very foolish, but the policeman thanked me for calling because they always want to investigate anything of a suspicious nature like that. He suggested kindly that I go up the next day and give her some advice about how to take care of the baby.

I had no advice to give, but I knew I had to go see her to apologize. And I'd rather have been struck dead than do it. I am so timid about knocking on doors anyway.

But the next morning I climbed the stairs to their apartment. I had been practicing a nice sincere little apology. When she opened the door, I burst out crying, "I'm sorry," I bawled.

She put her arms around me and drew me into the room. She, too, was sorry they had alarmed me. We had a nice visit together, but I never told any of my other friends in the building about it. I still felt too foolish.

At another time the tenant above me was a young man. One night he had company. I heard them talking loudly all night long. His company left at 5:30 A.M. and then someone started up the washer in the laundry room. There was just a wall between me and the laundry room, and my bed was against that wall. I knew he was the guilty one because I heard him open and close his door above me.

Snatching up my telephone, I dialed his number. When he answered I didn't even say "hello," or identify myself. I just burst out wrathfully, "Did you start that washer?"

"Audre, is that you?" he asked incredulously, then confessed that he had.

"You know better than to start it this early," I continued.

When he said he hadn't thought about it, I still poured it on, "There's a sign right on the wall above it. Can't you read?" Then I added my parting shot, "I knew it was you because you kept me awake all night with your talking!"

I'm usually such a *nice* agreeable person—really. He was quite taken aback and apologized profusely, but I hung up on him.

When the washer shut off, he waited until after eight o'clock (the proper time) to put the clothes in the dryer.

I knew he came home for lunch, so I watched for his car. When I heard him go into his apartment, I called him again and apologized. "I'm not apologizing for *what* I said," I told him, "I'm apologizing for the *way* I said it."

He was so nice and said that was all right. He understood.

"Well," I answered, "I could have been nicer about it. But I just don't *feel* very nice at 5:30 in the morning."

Just a Scribbler

I received a charming letter this week from a lady who apologized for being so brash as to write a famous author. I hope she was joking. I call myself a famous *unknown* author. Except that I really don't think of myself as an author at all. I'm just an old gal who has had a lifelong love affair with words and who loves to scribble in her spare time.

It all began when I was seven years old, while sitting at my desk in the little white Sunnyside schoolhouse in the country. I wrote my first poem there:

> *Green leaves in the summer,*
> *Red leaves in the fall,*
> *Hark, I hear a red bird*
> *Singing in the hall.*

After that there was no place to go but up. I couldn't do worse!

My sister, Elsie, and I spent more time playing with words than we did with dolls. I had an article published in the denominational church paper when I was 18, before I was married. When I was 22 I began writing short stories and poems for a Sunday School paper and continued for 20 or 25 years.

But it wasn't until I was 65 that I wrote my first book. When I was in my 20s I used to say that some day I was going to write a book titled *The Autobiography of a Nobody* about a common, ordinary person who had never set the world on fire.

Without realizing it, that is exactly what I've been doing. My life is an open book—four of them. This one could aptly be called *The Autobiography of a Nobody,* Volume 5.

Poetry is what I most enjoy scribbling. I call poetry "distilled literature." A friend once told me that I could say more in four lines than most people could say in a whole book. I doubt that—but here is another definition of what poetry is to me:

> *Poetry is the*
> *Music of the*
> *Soul—the*
> *Song the heart*
> *Sings in the*
> *Stillness of*
> *The night.*

I am often asked if I do a certain amount of writing every day and if I set aside certain hours just for that. My answer is "NO"—I write when I feel like it, and if I don't feel like it, there's no use trying. That definitely excludes me from being a dedicated writer. I've been told that writing is one-tenth inspiration and nine-tenths perspiration. OK, I'll share my inspiration with you—but not my sweat.

Another poem describes what I mean:

> *Sometimes my thoughts*
> *Are like fireflies—*
> *Beautiful—almost*
> *Brilliant—but*
> *Darting about so*
> *Swiftly that I*

*Find it hard to
Capture them and
Put them down on paper.*

*Again, they are
Like a mountain
Stream—flowing along
So smoothly and in
Such a rhythmic
Pattern that words
Come almost faster
Than my pen
Can write them.*

*And then at other
Times my brain
Becomes a snail—
Moving slowly,
Sluggishly—
Until at last
It crawls into
Its shell and
Takes a nap.*

I've been asked in interviews, "Why do you write?"

My only answer to that is, "Because I can't keep from it."

I've always done it, and I hope to continue as long as I live—whether for publication or pleasure. Poetry comes almost as natural as breathing, and as long as my little song-poems keep coming to me I'll scribble them down somewhere. It may be on the back of an old letter, or a grocery list, or even the church bulletin.

God gives to each of us different gifts and ministries. My prayer is that He can use whatever gift or talent He may have given me—no matter how small—and that His music will never stop playing in my soul, or His radiance cease to shine through me.

*Light my candle,
Lord, and may
Its tiny spark
Light up the
Hearts of lonely
Ones, crying
In the dark.*

Yesterday, Today, and Tomorrow

Most of my books are made up of memories, some recent, some long ago. But I would not want to give the impression of always harking back to the "good old days." No, indeed, some of those days weren't nearly as good in many ways as later ones. My yesterdays hold good memories, but I enjoy the creature comforts of today.

I'm willing to exchange five-cent ice cream cones and candy bars, circus tents, trains with steam engines that *really* whistled, and a few other things for what we have now. Who wouldn't trade a tub and washboard for an automatic washer or a clothes dryer instead of wet clothes hanging in the house on a rainy day? Some antique collector is welcome to my old wood range if he can find it. I'd rather keep my electric one and my little microwave oven. The list could go on and on.

Some say people aren't as friendly or helpful as they were in those good old days. I don't know where they live. Where I am folks are very friendly and always wanting to help.

I have friends who think they have found a treasure when they buy an old kerosene lamp at a flea market. *They* never had to fill several every day, wash the chimneys until they shone, and trim the wicks so their "treasure" wouldn't get all smoked up again.

Farms are specialized today. When I was a farmer's wife we raised pigs, chickens, and cows besides corn, wheat, oats, and other grain. Now dairy farms are equipped with the latest, most effective (and *easiest*) ways of cleaning all the equipment. I (a 115 pound weakling) had to scrub 10-gallon cream cans by hand. And there was that monster (the cream separator) with a huge bowl that we poured the milk in. Then around and around and around we turned it while cream poured out of one spout and the skim milk another. A marvelous invention. I learned in high school General Science that it worked on the principle of centrifugal force. Amazing what I learned in school. Living with it, I learned to hate it.

Besides the big bowl, there was a string of cone-shaped cylinders that had to be washed one by one every day. They were fastened on a rod together but loose enough so you could wash each separately. That is a poor description, but those who have used them know what I mean. Those who have never used them—be grateful!

For several years after we left the farm (I was the one who persuaded my husband that God wanted us to move), at the top of each day's praise list was, "Thank You, God, because I don't have to wash the separator today."

I hadn't intended to start sounding so negative. There are many good memories of those days, and I wouldn't want to forget them. I'm glad I had them all.

Our past, present, and future cannot really be separated —though some may try. They blend together into a pattern and that pattern is life. I want to remember the past, live and enjoy today, and dream for the future—while the music keeps on playing!

> *He who turns his back*
> *On all his yesterdays*

Loses half his wealth—
Today and yesterday
Are all he really has—
Tomorrow's but a dream.

Yes—tomorrow's but a dream
So let my dreams be full of hope—
Not stifled by the past
Nor yet content with laurels won today—
Be they great or small—
Tomorrow's still a dream
So let me dream big dreams—
And should there be no tomorrow,
Today will have been happier
For the dreaming.

P.S.

Impressions of a first cruise from the viewpoint of a "past-the-60s" lady.

All Cruisin', No Boozin'

This chapter is sort of a postscript to the rest of the book. I thought it was finished. Then I went on a Caribbean cruise with a group of Christians for a Celebration at Sea.

Doris and I wondered if we would make it to Miami in time to embark. We started early the day before, flying from Portland. All went well until we got to Atlanta. The terminal there had been closed most of the day, but we landed without incident.

Getting away was another matter. The crew changed there, and we had to wait for over two hours for our pilot to get there over icy roads. I thought Atlanta was always warm. But it was 25° that day with snow and ice everywhere.

There were planes ahead of us being deiced for takeoff. Over five hours after landing there we were finally able to take off. Other travelers weren't so fortunate. Some had to be flown from Miami to Jamaica to catch the cruise later.

We had some difficulty finding our luggage in Miami, but after two hours it came through the chute. I was so exhausted from standing all that time that, when Doris went to phone the hotel of our arrival, I decided I just had to sit down. It was not a wise decision. I sat down on my suitcase. It flipped over backward and so did I. A kind skycap scraped me up off the floor, and we made it to the hotel after 2 A.M. Edna had been waiting for us since 7:30 P.M. as the three of us were rooming together there and on the ship.

But the cruise was worth it all. It was fabulous plus. For the talent show a friend suggested that I write a humorous poem about the cruise. Neither Ken nor I realized what a terrific publicity stunt that would turn out to be. From then on I was besieged by requests for copies. Finally I promised that I'd try to add it to this book—and that seemed to satisfy. Well . . . that should be good for quite a few sales!

So here it is, like a cherry on top of an ice cream sundae.

When I read it that night, I added comments now and then as I will now.

> *Christians from various denominations*
> *Came together for a celebration.*
>
> *From all parts of the country they came*
> *To celebrate in Jesus' name.*
>
> *They came from the south, north, east, and west.*
> *One even flew over the cuckoo's nest.*
>
> *They battled the ice and cold and snow,*
> *Because they were all so anxious to go.*
>
> *January 8—day of embarkation,*
> *All our hearts were filled with elation.*
>
> *We gave them our cards and, a few minutes later,*
> *I missed my step and fell up the escalator.*
>
> *No sooner did the cruise begin*
> *Than we had a life jacket drill that about did me in.*

(I didn't have just an inflated vest. Mine was a heavy jacket that went clear around and had to be tied in three places in front. It must have been made for a tall person because it covered my nose until I couldn't breathe.

(When we got up on deck it was *hot* and *muggy*. There were three lines in my group, and I was on the inside one. Everyone around me was about a foot higher than I. I thought my cruise would end right then with death by suffocation.)

The captain's gala dinner was a delight;
The ladies dressed up fit to kill that night.

We had church in Jamaica on the Lord's Day;
God's presence was there in a beautiful way.

Afterward some of us took a tour;
We saw that the economy was very poor.

At San Blas Islands some went by canoe;
On one of the isles we had a barbeque.

I ate frog legs, snails, and caviar;
I ate way too much, by far.

Then I piled lobster and baked Alaska on top;
I got so full I was ready to pop.

And all of those gorgeous buffets they served—
No wonder I grew a few more curves.

How I could grow more is hard to figure,
But the ones I had kept growing bigger.

When I stepped off the plane, I expected some imp,
To yell, "Look, Mom, there's a blimp!"

Our cabin steward's name was Kwan—
I really enjoyed being waited on.

And in the lounge and on the deck,
I was adopted as his grandmother by a fellow named Paek.

(Paek is Korean. He wrote his name for me in Chinese, Korean, and English. Then he said, "My name is Paek, my father's name is Paek, and my son's name is Paek. We are *impeccable!*")

*When the sea turned rough instead of serene,
We saw a lot of tipsy Nazarenes.*

*Also some Wesleyans and Frees,
Even Baptists and Lutherans seemed to sway in the breeze.*

*We'd rock and we'd roll and nearly collapse,
Almost landing in people's laps.*

*We'd swing and we'd sway, we'd teeter and totter,
And wobble around a lot more than we oughter.*

*But the funniest ones to watch, by far,
Were the ones who came staggering out of the bar.*

*They acted like they feared the boat would sink,
But they looked like they'd had too much to drink.*

*Before I cause some consternation,
I'll offer a word of explanation.*

*We only went to the bar to frolic,
All of the drinks were nonalcoholic.*

*I couldn't judge by looks, no siree—
Cause the next one who lurched out might have been me.*

*Other things can cause a person to fall
Besides drinking alcohol.*

*The roll of the ship really helped me to sleep,
I loved being rocked in the cradle of the deep.*

*But walking was a different matter,
If I fell—great would be the splatter.*

*I wished my legs had bones, not jelly,
I expected any minute to fall on my—stomach.*

*I'd never been on a cruise before
So I wasn't acquainted with ship lore.*

*When I saw little white bags on the rails in the hall,
I didn't know what they were for at all.*

*Then it penetrated my head so thick—
They were "barf bags" for those who got sick.*

*When the cruise ended and we split the scene
I feared we'd all be addicted to Dramamine.*

*I thought the showers were rather small;
I didn't quite fit into ours at all.*

*Taking a bath to the swing and sway
Of the ship, as it rocked, was like modern ballet.*

*And it didn't help much—that's for certain
If you lost your balance and grabbed the curtain.*

*We had a great celebration, I'd say—
We'd laugh and we'd talk, we'd sing and we'd pray.*

*We took lots of pictures and played games,
And walked the deck till our legs were lame.*

*We may have worn blisters on our feet
But, through it all, we'd EAT, EAT, EAT!*

*It was a cruise I will never forget,
And I wasn't ready to come home yet.*

It was truly a cruise to remember. One of the interesting incidents was when we were anchored near the San Blas Islands. Early in the morning whole families of the Cuna Indians who live there in bamboo thatched houses came in canoes and lingered all day on each side of our ship. The youngsters would yell, "Money, money!" perhaps the only English word they knew except "dollah."

I enjoyed watching the children dive for the coins I dropped overboard. They looked like little frogs with their arms and legs outspread, swimming underwater.

All things must end . . . even our cruise. We disembarked around 10:30 A.M. By evening the Galileo would sail with another shipload of passengers.

No doubt Mario is still trying to tempt some overweight female to indulge in extra desserts. And Liberato—almost as young as my grandson—is escorting other elderly fat ladies out of the dining room, placing a gentle kiss on the cheek at parting. May it warm their wrinkled old hearts as much as it did mine.

The cruise is ended—but the music will keep on playing for a long, long time.